CONTENTS

5 SIMPLE WAYS TO STRENGTHEN YOUR MARRIAGE

... When You're Stuck at Home Together

Gary Chapman

NORTHFIELD PUBLISHING

CHICAGO

Scriptures taken from the Holy Bible, New International Version®, NIV®. Copyright © 1973, 1978, 1984, 2011 by Biblica, Inc.™ Used by permission of Zondervan. All rights reserved worldwide. www.zondervan.com The "NIV" and "New International Version" are trademarks registered in the United States Patent and Trademark Office by Biblica, Inc.™

Edited by Connor Sterchi
Interior and cover design: Erik M. Peterson
Cover illustration of couple copyright © 2018 by CSA-Printstock/iStock (1003475380). All rights reserved.

ISBN: 978-0-8024-2332-0

We hope you enjoy this book from Northfield Publishing. Our goal is to provide high-quality, thought-provoking books and products that connect truth to your real needs and challenges. For more information on other books and products that will help you with all your important relationships, go to northfieldpublishing .com or write to:

Northfield Publishing
820 N. LaSalle Boulevard
Chicago, IL 60610

1 3 5 7 9 10 8 6 4 2

Printed in the United States of America

INTRODUCTION

S ome have said that we are all in the same ship as we face the turbulent seas of COVID-19. That is not true. We are all in our own ship. Some of you have small children in your ship. Others have college students who have gotten back into your ship. For many, it is simply you and your spouse. You may be healthy, or one (or both) of you may be sick. You may be working from home, or you may no longer have a job. No, we are not in the same ship. However, for all of us, the dynamics of life are very different than they were before the storm.

Some are predicting that the divorce rate will increase in America when the "shelter-in-place" orders are lifted.

Reports indicate that is exactly what happened in China when the quarantine was lifted. Let me suggest that quarantines do not cause divorce—people do. If the marriage relationship was fractured before the pandemic, then being confined together simply reveals what was already true. If the marriage was healthy, then the couple may even thrive during the lockdown.

This book is addressed to all married couples, healthy or unhealthy. Your marriage can be better. Marriage relationships are not static. They either get better or worse with each passing day. Has the COVID-19 pandemic changed our environment? Without question! For many, it has created financial pressure, which may stimulate anxiety. If children are in the picture, they are now "ever present," 24/7. Many parents are telling me they have a much deeper appreciation for school teachers since the schools have been closed. Our daily routines have been changed, which often creates stress. But none of these changes make or break a marriage.

As humans, we are extremely adaptable. We choose our attitude and we choose our behavior. We do not choose our emotions. We may feel frustrated, angry, disappointed, lonely, or we may feel happy, excited, loved, and secure.

While emotions tend to influence us, they need not control our behavior. Our society has exalted emotions as the guiding star for life. You will hear people say, "I have got to be true to my emotions." Or "I have to follow my heart." So they make decisions based on their emotions. If their emotions are negative, often these decisions have detrimental results in their marriage and to their children. Don't misunderstand me; emotions are an important part of our humanity, but they should not control our behavior.

In times of crisis, we need to rediscover the power of our attitude and our behavior. We are far more likely to make wise decisions if we choose a positive attitude. Our attitude is what we choose to believe. A negative attitude says:

> "Our marriage can never be better."
> "People can't change."
> "This crisis is going to destroy us."

All of those attitudes are myths that grow out of our negative emotions. A positive attitude says:

"This is a hard time, but we are going to make it."

"We are going to use this present crisis to enrich our marriage."

"We need to change some things, and I am going to be the first to change."

"I choose to use this time as an opportunity to enrich our marriage and the lives of our children."

What I want to do in this short book is share five ways you can enhance your marriage and create a better environment in which to raise your children. If you have children, there is no better gift than to give them a model of a mom and dad who have a loving, caring, supportive relationship. I believe you can have that kind of marriage. So whether you are in a healthy marriage or a struggling marriage, let's make it better while we are processing the current crisis.

The suggestions I am going to make grow out of forty years of counseling couples. I have seen marriages saved by applying these simple practices, and I have seen good marriages become great marriages by learning these skills. The short chapters that follow will give you five ways to enhance your marriage. Ideally, both you and your spouse can read a chapter and then discuss how to apply the material in your marriage. I'm fully aware that you cannot make your spouse join you in reading and discussing. However, if you both read and decide to practice what you read, it will move the marriage in a positive direction. I predict that you will begin to see a change in your spouse's behavior as they observe the changes that are taking place in you. All of us are influenced by the way other people treat us. Don't underestimate the power of a positive influence.

CHAPTER 1

CALL A TRUCE ON THROWING VERBAL BOMBS

The old saying "Sticks and stones may break my bones, but words can never hurt me" is totally false. Words have great power to hurt. The truth is found in an ancient Hebrew proverb: "The tongue has the power of life and death."[1] You can kill your relationship or give it life by the way you talk. Everything we say is either a bomb or a balm. Bombs destroy. Balm is an aromatic oil or ointment that is soothing and healing. Harsh, cruel, condemning words are like bombs exploding in the heart of the recipient. Kind, loving, affirming words are like an ointment of healing to the heart of the one who receives them.

Unfortunately, all of us sometimes throw verbal bombs at our spouse. Such words are often spoken in anger. We say things like: "I can't count on you for anything." "You are just like your father/mother—totally irresponsible." "Would you put that phone down and listen to me?" "When you take a walk, why don't you take Johnny with you? He likes to get outside, and I need a little relief." "I don't think you would ever touch me if I didn't initiate it." "You know I don't like salmon. So why did you fix it?" "You are driving me crazy playing video games all day." I could go on, but you get the picture.

These verbal bombs are coming out of our anger. Anger is the emotion we feel when we believe we have been treated unfairly. Often our anger is legitimate; we have been mistreated. Such anger should lead to lovingly confronting our spouse and seeking reconciliation. (We will talk about this in chapter 2.) However, much of our anger is distorted. Our spouse did not mistreat us; they simply did not do what we thought they should have done. Or they did not do it the way we wanted it done. For example, I remember getting angry with my wife about the way she loaded a dishwasher. I am an organized person, and I load a dishwasher in an organized manner. Thus, nothing gets broken and everything gets clean. Karolyn loads a dishwasher like she was playing Frisbee. So, in anger, I gave her a harsh lecture. Did that help our marriage? No! She got angry at me for the way I talked to her. A verbal bomb usually stimulates a retaliation. I bomb her and she bombs me and we are destroying what we wanted most: a loving marriage.

When we are thrown together 24/7, personality differences may surface more often and more intensely. The question is how will we deal with these irritations? By nature, some people lash out in anger with harsh, hurtful words. Others clam up and give their spouse the "silent treatment." Neither of these enhance the relationship. Life-giving words are a much better choice. What if I had said to Karolyn, "Honey, I really appreciate the fact that you load the dishwasher. Is that something you enjoy doing, or would you rather have me load it? I'm open to that if it would help you." Can you feel the soothing, healing balm of those words?

I can hear someone saying, "That is just not natural.

No one talks like that when they are upset." It is true that when we are feeling angry, our natural response is to lob a verbal bomb. But doing what "comes natural" does not enhance a marriage. Learning to control our anger and not let anger control us is a huge lesson in having a healthy marriage. Once you throw the bomb, it explodes. Such verbal explosions never move us in the right direction. That is why I am suggesting: *call a truce on throwing verbal bombs.* Whether throwing verbal bombs is a "way of life" in your marriage or only an "occasional" event, would you consider "calling a truce"? Now that many of us are spending more time in the same geographical space, we have a wonderful opportunity to initiate a truce.

A truce is an agreement that we will halt the bombing and create an atmosphere in which we can talk about our relationship and seek to make it what we both desire—a place of peace and not warfare. Throughout history, a number of international conflicts have been solved when each party was willing to call a truce and negotiate. I believe that many marriages could also find peace, but first we must stop the bombing.

What if you are reading this book alone and your spouse is not willing to join you? All is not hopeless! If you decide that you want to change the atmosphere in your marriage and are willing to make an agreement with yourself to stop throwing bombs from your side, at least there would be fewer bombs exploding in your house. When you don't retaliate to your spouse's bombs, he or she may run out of ammunition. It is hard to keep shooting when no one is returning fire.

Now comes the second step. What if during this truce you begin to replace verbal bombs with verbal balms? What if you seek to replace complaining with gratitude? What if you start looking for things you appreciate about your spouse? I believe if you "look," you will likely "find"! Now I did have one lady say to me, "I know it would be good if I could give my husband some positive words, but to be honest with you, I can't think of anything good to say about him." I thought a moment and said, "Well, does he ever take a shower?" To which she responded, "Well yes." "How often?" I asked. "Well, every day," she replied. I said, "If I were you, I would start there. Imagine saying to him, 'Honey, I don't think I have ever told you this, but I appreciate the fact that you take a shower every day. I understand that there are men who don't, and I really appreciate that about you.'" I have never met a man or a woman that I could not find something about them for which to give thanks. I'm sure that your spouse is no exception.

For some of us, speaking words of gratitude comes easy. We received affirming words growing up, and we learned as a child to say "thank you" when someone did something for us. We seldom left the table without saying, "Thank you Mom/Dad for lunch." If this was our childhood experience, then verbally expressing gratitude to our spouse probably comes rather natural for us. However, there are others who seldom heard affirming words growing up, and as adults, we do not naturally speak words of gratitude. Whether easy or difficult, all of us can learn to express gratitude.

A husband once told me he did not know how to express thanks to his wife. "It just doesn't seem natural to me," he said. "I can understand that," I said. I knew he was an avid golfer. So I said to him, "I expect when you first started playing golf it did not seem natural to you. Am I right?" "You are right about that. I was the worst beginner you could ever imagine. I lost dozens of golf balls in the lake." "So how did you learn to play golf?" I asked. "Little by little," he said. "I just kept trying, and of course

I had a good coach." "Then I will be your coach if you are willing to try," I said. "Little by little it will begin to feel more natural, but you have to keep trying." He agreed, and eventually he became an award-winning husband.

One of the things I suggested to this husband was to get a "gratitude" notebook. On the first page, he wrote: Things I Appreciate About My Wife. I asked him to write three things on page one this week and bring them back to me next week. Admittedly, from my perspective, they were pretty generic.

1. She is a good cook.
2. She is a good mother.
3. She is a good school teacher.

But we started where he was. I wrote the following in his gratitude notebook beside each of his statements:

1. Honey, I know I haven't told you this very often, but you are an excellent cook, and I really appreciate all the meals you prepare.

2. Mary (his wife's name), I've been thinking about what a wonderful mother you are to our children, and

I want to thank you for all you do for them.

3. How did your teaching go this week? I bet the parents of your students really appreciate you. From all I hear, you are a great teacher.

Then I asked him to read each of these aloud to me. He read rather haltingly, but he read them. "Now this week, I want you to stand in front of a mirror and read each of these statements aloud at least twice a day," I said. "That's all?" he asked. "That's all for this week," I said.

The next week I asked him to share each of these statements without looking at his notebook. He did fairly well. "Okay, now here is your assignment for the next three weeks," I said. "I want you to share with Mary one of these statements each week. You choose the time and place, but each week you express your gratitude to her for one of these three things." "This is going to be hard," he said. "I know, but a good golfer like you can do it," I said. We both laughed as he said, "I'll try it." "That's all it takes," I said as he walked out of my office.

Three weeks later he walked into my office with a smile on his face. "How did it go?" I asked. "Last week, when I made my third statement, she said to me, 'What's going on with you? I've never heard you give me so many compliments.'" "And what did you say?" I asked. "I told her that I was just trying to learn how to express to her how much I appreciate her." She said, "That is so sweet of you. I love you so much." "She had not said that in a long time," he said. "It felt good." Again, I was reminded of the power of speaking words of gratitude.

From there we moved on to broaden the scope of speaking positive words to his wife. We focused on things he liked about her personality. He came up with a pretty good list. Then he started thanking her for the things she did for him, things he had just taken for granted. He started noticing her clothes and telling her how nice she looked. He thanked her for putting up with his obsession with golf and not making him feel guilty when he went to the club. Within nine months he was an all-star husband in Mary's eyes.

So maybe expressing appreciation to your spouse comes easy for you. Or maybe it is extremely difficult for you. If so, I hope this story will encourage you to get started. Don't allow your past experience to destroy your present reality. Now that you are spending more time together, let's learn to create a more positive relationship by learning to replace verbal bombs with verbal balms.

MAKING IT PRACTICAL

1. If both of you are willing, sign a truce. If only one of you is willing, then commit yourself and sign the truce.

   Put the following words on a sheet of paper, which each of you can sign and date:

   > We know that harsh, critical words are hurtful to our relationship. Therefore, we commit ourselves to calling a truce on such words. We will not only seek to stop throwing verbal bombs at each other, but we will seek to replace negative words with positive words of appreciation.

2. Start your own "gratitude" notebook.

   This week, list three things you appreciate about your spouse.

   Add two additional things each week for six weeks.

3. Seek to verbally express appreciation to your spouse at least once a week.

4. When you fail and speak harshly or critically to your spouse, first calm down, and then come back and apologize. (More about this in chapter 2.)

TEAR DOWN EMOTIONAL WALLS

Marriages do not flourish when there are emotional walls between the husband and wife. Walls are built one block at a time. A wife said, "Yesterday he told me I was lazy because I did not replace the trash bag when I took the old one out. That really hurt." "Did he come back and apologize?" I asked. "No, and he won't," she said. An emotional block has just been placed between the two of them. It can be little or big offenses, but each failure that is not dealt with will put another block in the wall. Many couples have built long, thick walls between them. These are the couples that contemplate divorce or decide to live in the same house as roommates, each living their own life. Walls are not removed with the passing of time. When we are confined to close quarters, the wall makes life much more difficult.

Of course, not all couples have walls between them. However, all couples offend each other from time to time. Sometimes it is intentional and sometimes unintentional, but each offense puts an emotional block between them. There is only one way to remove the block: apology and forgiveness. If they fail to apologize and forgive, the offense becomes the first block in a wall. However, if they genuinely apologize and forgive, there will be no wall. The relationship moves forward in a healthy manner.

I believe that apology and forgiveness are essential for a long-term healthy marriage. I say they are essential because there are no perfect husbands or wives. All of us fail from time to time. One man raised his hand when the speaker asked, "Does anyone know of a perfect husband?" He said, "My wife's first husband." My observation is that if there are any perfect husbands, they are deceased, and most of them got perfect after they died. We don't have to be perfect to have healthy marriages, but we do need to deal effectively with our failures.

So let's talk about apologies and forgiveness. Where do we learn to apologize? Typically from our parents or someone who served as our parents. Little Johnny pushes his sister, and his mother says, "Johnny, don't do that to your sister! Go tell her you are sorry." So Johnny says, "I'm sorry," even if he's not. He is now twenty-four and married. When he offends his wife, what will he say? Likely, "I'm sorry." We discovered in our research that about 10 percent of the population almost never apologizes for anything, and most of them are men. They learned it from their fathers who said, "Real men don't apologize." I say to those men, "Your father may have been a good man, but he had bad information. Real men do apologize. In fact, it is real men who both apologize and forgive."

Because we had different parents, we have different ideas about what it means to apologize. Mary's mother taught her to say, "I was wrong. I should not have done that. I hope you will forgive me." So when her husband Johnny says, "I'm sorry," she does not see that as a sincere apology. What all of us are asking when someone apologizes to us is, "Are they sincere?" If we judge them to be sincere, it is much easier to forgive them. However, we judge sincerity by how they apologize. In our research, we discovered several ways in which people apologize. One is by expressing regret, often with the words "I'm sorry." But don't ever stop with those two words. Tell them what you are sorry for. "I'm sorry that I lost my temper and yelled at you." And don't ever use the word "but." "I'm sorry that I lost my temper and yelled at you, but if you had not . . . then I would not have . . ." Now you are no longer apologizing. You are blaming them for your bad behavior.

Another common way to apologize is to accept responsibility for your behavior. That is what Mary was doing when she admitted: "I was wrong. I should not have done that." For others, a sincere apology always seeks to make restitution. "What can I do to make this right?" They want to make amends for their behavior. Still others want to hear you express the desire to change your behavior. "I don't like this about me. I don't want to keep doing this. I know I did the same thing last month. Can you help me find a way so I won't do this again?" A wife shared this illustration: "My husband lost his temper with our baby. The baby was crying, and he did everything he knew to do, and the baby continued crying. He lost his temper and started yelling at our baby. I ran into our bedroom sobbing. Ten minutes later, he knocked on the door and asked if he could come in. He walked in with tears and told me how badly he felt about what he had done and said that he never wanted to do that again. We talked and came up with a simple plan. If he ever felt he was about to lose his temper with one of our children, he would say to me, 'Honey, I'm hot. I've got to take a walk.' I knew what that meant, and I would take over. He would walk around the block and then return and say, 'Okay, I think I'm under control. What can I do to help you?' That was eight years ago, and he has never lost his temper with one of our children since. He has taken several walks, but he has never lost his temper.

One of our problems in offering a meaningful apology is that we judge sincerity by what we think they should be saying. They often are not saying what we want to hear, likely because their parents taught them a different way to apologize. So while you have more time together, this would be a good time to share with each other what you consider to be a sincere apology. You will likely discover why you have felt their apologies of the past have been rather lame. Now you can learn how to express your apology in the future in terms that are more meaningful to your spouse. You can also come to accept the sincerity of your spouse's apology since you now know that in childhood they learned a different way of expressing apology than you learned.

FORGIVENESS

Apology alone will not remove the emotional barrier created by our offense. There must be a response to an apology. The healthy response is to forgive. Forgiveness is a choice. If you choose not to forgive, then the barrier remains, and your relationship is hindered. Forgiveness means to pardon or to remove the barrier. Forgiveness is expressing the choice to not hold the offense against your spouse. You will not make them pay for this the rest of their life. You will remove the barrier so that your relationship moves forward.

It is important to know that there are some things that forgiveness does not do. Forgiveness does not destroy the memory of the offense. You may have heard people say, "If you have not forgotten, you have not forgiven." That is not true. Everything that has ever happened to us is stored in the human brain, and sometimes even after we have forgiven, the memory comes back to the mind. Nor does forgiveness remove all of the painful emotions. When the memory returns, often it is accompanied by emotions. Hurt, anger, sorrow, and other emotions may grip us. What do we do with these memories and emotions? I believe we remind ourselves that our spouse has apologized, and we have chosen to forgive them. Therefore, I will not allow the memory and the emotions to control my behavior. I will seek to do something kind and loving for my spouse today. Your loving words or actions will speak deeply to your spouse, and you will feel good about doing something positive in spite of your negative feelings.

Another thing that forgiveness does not do is rebuild trust. She sits in my office with tears as she says, "My husband was sexually unfaithful to me. He broke off the relationship and apologized to me. I have forgiven him and agreed to work on our marriage, but I have to be honest, I do not trust him." I said, "I am empathetic with that. Forgiveness does not restore trust. Forgiveness opens the door to the possibility that trust can be reborn. Trust is reborn over time as your husband is trustworthy." My advice to her husband was to allow her full access to his life. He might say to her, "My computer is yours anytime you want to look at it and so is my phone. If I tell you

I am going to the gym, it is fine with me if you want to come by and see if I am where I said I would be. I am through with deceit. I have hurt you deeply, and I do not want to hurt you again. My life is an open book." If he takes that approach, chances are his wife will come to trust him again. In the meanwhile, they can continue to rebuild their marriage by practicing the five things we are discussing in this book.

I think you can see why I am suggesting that apology and forgiveness are essential to having a long-term healthy marriage. So if you entered this pandemic season with a wall between the two of you, this would be an ideal time to tear the wall down. Make a list of all the things you can remember where you failed your spouse. Then say to them, "I have been thinking about us, and I know I have hurt you in many ways. I feel badly about what I have done. You do not deserve the way I have treated you. I made a list of some of my failures that came to mind, and if you would allow me, I would like to share these and ask if you can find it in your heart to forgive me. I would like to try to make up for all the pain I have caused you. I know I can't undo these things, but I do want to change the future. I'm also open for you to share anything that I don't have on this list. I really want to deal with my failures. I want to be the husband/wife you deserve." Such an honest apology may be the first step in tearing down the wall between you. Your spouse may be willing to forgive you. However, they may want some time to think about what you are saying and to process their own emotions and thoughts. Remember, forgiveness is a choice just as apology is a choice. Both are necessary to remove the wall.

Many of you do not have a wall between you. You are dealing with your failures as they occur. Hopefully this chapter will help you understand apology and forgiveness a little better and become even more effective in dealing with your failures. With the stress of the present crisis, you may indeed say and do things that are hurtful. The sooner you apologize and forgive, the more likely you are to also apply the other suggestions you'll see in the following chapters.

If your spouse is someone who seldom (if ever) apologizes, what are you to do? I believe you kindly, lovingly confront them with their offense. You might say, "If I had something that was bothering me, would this be a good time to share it with you?" When they are willing to listen, you can say, "I may be misreading this, but I would like to share with you something that really hurt me." Then you proceed to share with them what they said or did that hurt you. Then you might say, "Can you understand why that hurt me? If I am misunderstanding the situation, could you please explain it to me?" This is what I mean by kindly, lovingly confronting your spouse.

Your spouse has a choice of explaining or apologizing for their behavior. Either way, you are now free to remove the emotional barrier and your relationship can move forward. Making every effort to remove the barrier and not allow a wall to be built between you is the path of wisdom. You cannot make your spouse apologize, just as they cannot make you forgive them, but you can lovingly confront. This approach is far more productive than holding the hurt inside and letting the anger build. This leads to an eventual explosion, and then you will be the one who needs to apologize. To have a healthy marriage, you must share with each other when you feel you have been wronged. If the two of you can agree on this approach, you will have taken a huge step forward in revitalizing your marriage.

MAKING IT PRACTICAL

1. If both of you have read this chapter together, have a "sit down" time, and share with each other your concept of a sincere apology. Talk about how you have processed failures in the past and how you might be more effective in the future.

2. Ask each other, "Is there any time in the past when I have hurt you and failed to apologize? If so, I would like to deal with it, because I want us to have a healthy marriage."

3. Ask each other, "Has something happened recently in the stress of life where I have hurt you? If so, I want to apologize."

4. Ask each other, "Do you feel that, in the past, I have forgiven you when you apologized?"

5. Ask each other, "What else can we learn from this chapter?"

If your spouse has not read this chapter and is not interested in talking about apology and forgiveness, why not begin by apologizing for your own failures? Perhaps you feel that your spouse is 95 percent of the problem; then apologize for your 5 percent. Your example alerts your spouse that something is going on in your heart and mind. In the past, they may have heard critical, condemning words from you, but now they are hearing you apologize. If you develop a pattern of apology when you say or do something hurtful, you are having a positive influence on your spouse. In time, you may hear them begin to apologize. Don't underestimate the power of influence.

CHAPTER 3

DISCOVER AND SPEAK EACH OTHER'S LOVE LANGUAGE

Some of you may have read my book *The 5 Love Languages: The Secret to Love That Lasts*. It has sold over thirteen million copies and has been translated and published in over fifty languages around the world. Many couples have told me that the book actually saved their marriage. If you have read the book, what I am sharing in this chapter will be a review. It will help you get the love language of your spouse back on the "front burner" of your thinking during this time of crisis. If you have not read the original book, this brief synopsis will be an introduction to the concept and how you can revitalize your marriage by discovering and speaking your spouse's primary love language.

Almost everyone agrees that the deepest emotional need we have as humans is the need to feel loved by the significant people in our lives. If we are married and genuinely feel loved by our spouse, life is beautiful. Even in times of crisis, we can process the added pressures of life much easier. However, if we do not feel loved by our spouse, life can begin to look pretty dark, and in times of uncertainty, our marriage can be threatened.

Most of us can remember the season of life in which we met each other and "fell in love." The high euphoric feelings carried us along without much conscious effort. We viewed each other as incredibly wonderful. Our parents may have pointed out the flaws of our lover, but we did not see them. One mother said to her daughter, "Honey, have you considered he hasn't had a steady job in five years?" To which the daughter replied, "Give him a break, Mom. He is just waiting for the right opportunity." We see the world through rose-colored glasses when we are in love.

No one told me that the average life span of the "in love" euphoria is two years. My wife and I had dated two years before we got married, so I came down off the high pretty soon after we got married. I remember thinking, "I've lost it. I wonder if I have made a mistake in getting married." Of course, I did not tell my wife, but I definitely had the thought. I wish I had known then what I know now. There are two stages of romantic love. The first stage is what I have just described, commonly called "falling in love" or "being in love." It takes little effort on our part. We just "go with the flow" and enjoy our relationship. The second stage is far more intentional.

I remember talking with a young lady in a Chicago airport who was going to visit her fiancé at the Great Lakes Naval Training Center. She asked me about my vocation. I told her that I was a marriage counselor and tried to help people work on their marriage. "Why do you have to work on a marriage?" she asked, in all sincerity. I knew she was in love, and the thought of having to work on a relationship was foreign to her thinking.

The fact is, we do have to work on a marriage if we are going to keep romantic love alive after the "in love" euphoria. The difficulty in doing this is that we have assumed what makes me feel loved will also make the other person feel loved. That is a false assumption. I remember the first time I encountered this reality in my counseling office many years ago. I was counseling a couple that had been married to each other for thirty years. The wife said, "I just don't feel any love coming from him. We are like two roommates living in the same house. I feel so lonely inside, and I don't know how much longer I can go on like this."

I looked at her husband and he said, "I don't understand her. I do everything I can to show her that I love her, and she still says she doesn't feel loved. I don't know what else to do." So I asked, "What do you do to show your love to her?" He said, "Well, I get home from work before she does, so I start the evening meal. Sometimes I have it ready when she gets home. If not, she will help me, and after we eat, I wash the dishes. Every Thursday night I vacuum the floor, and every Saturday I wash the car, mow the grass, and help her with the laundry." He went on, and I was beginning to wonder: "What does this woman do?" It sounded to me like he was doing everything. I looked back at his wife, and she said, "He's right. He is a hard-working man, but we don't ever talk. We have not talked in twenty years. He is always washing dishes, mowing grass, walking the dog, or doing something else." Do you get the picture? Here was a husband who was doing everything he could think of to express love to his wife and a wife who did not feel loved. After that encounter, I had numerous couples share similar stories.

Eventually, I decided to read several years of notes that I had taken while counseling couples, looking for an answer to this question: When someone said, "I don't feel loved by my spouse," what did they want? Or what were they complaining about? Their answers fell into five categories, and I later called them the five love languages. So I started using that concept in my counseling. I would say to the husband, "If you want her to feel loved, you have got to express love in her love language." And to the wife, "If you want him to feel loved, you must express love in his love language." I would help them discover each other's love language and challenge them to go home and speak it. Sometimes they would come back in only three weeks and say, "This is changing everything. The whole emotional climate is different now." So here is a brief summary of the five love languages. As you read, think about which one is most important to you.

Words of Affirmation—using words to affirm your spouse. "You look nice in that dress." "I really appreciate what you did for me." "Do you know one of the things I like about you? Your smile. When you smile at me, the whole world looks beautiful." "One of the things I like about you is your integrity. I know that you will always tell me the truth." The words may focus on how they look, something they have done for you, or some personality trait. You are simply using words to express your love. You can speak the words, write the words, or even sing the words. Remember the ancient Hebrew proverb we quoted in chapter 1? "The tongue has the power of life and death."

For some people, Words of Affirmation is their primary love language. If you give them affirming words, they thrive. They feel deeply loved. If, on the other hand, you give them harsh, critical words, it is like a dagger in their heart.

Acts of Service—doing something for your spouse that you know they would like for you to do. Cooking a meal is an act of service. Washing dishes, folding towels, watering the lawn, washing the car, or changing the baby's diaper are all acts of service. The husband whom I described earlier was speaking this love language. Many wives would feel deeply loved if their husbands did these acts of service. His problem was that he was not married to one of these women. Acts of Service was not his wife's love language. He was, in fact, expressing love, but it was missing the target.

Have you heard the old saying, "Actions speak louder than words?" That is true if Acts of Service is your love language. However, it is not true for everyone.

Receiving Gifts—it is universal to give gifts as an expression of love. My academic background before I studied counseling was cultural anthropology, the study of cultures. We have never discovered a culture where gift giving is not an expression of love. The gift says to the recipient, "They were thinking about me. Look what they got for me."

The gift need not be expensive. I've sometimes suggested to husbands that they follow the example of their young children who pick dandelions in the yard and give them to their mothers. I'm not suggesting dandelions, but flowers from the yard. If you don't have flowers in your yard, look at your neighbor's yard. (Ask your neighbor, don't steal them.) One husband told me that he was taking a walk and saw a bird feather. He picked it up and took it home and gave it to his wife with these words: "Honey, I found this feather while I was walking, and I thought of you. You are the wind beneath my wings, girl, and I love you." He hit a home run because his wife's primary love language was Words of Affirmation, and her secondary language was Receiving Gifts.

If Receiving Gifts is your spouse's primary love language, I suggest you make a list of the kind of things in which they show interest. If you are watching a TV ad and your spouse says, "That would be nice," get the phone number and surprise her/him a few days later when it arrives at the door. If you are newly married and know that your spouse's love language is Receiving Gifts, but you have no clue as to where to begin, ask her sister or his brother for ideas. They likely know the kind of things that would be meaningful to them. If money is tight in this season, your spouse will not expect expensive gifts. Their favorite candy bar may be the perfect gift. Remember, it's the thought that counts.

Quality Time—giving your spouse your undivided attention. I do not mean sitting on the couch watching television (something else has your attention). Nor do I mean sitting in the same room while both of you are looking at your laptops. I'm talking about things like sitting on the couch or in your favorite chairs, with the television off, computers down, not answering your phones, but rather looking at each other and talking and listening. They have your undivided attention. Or taking a walk and talking as you walk. Or, in your former life, it might have been going to your favorite restaurant, assuming that you were talking and listening to each other. (Maybe that day will return soon.) I have been amazed in the past several years to observe couples sitting in the restaurant with both of them on their smartphones. I hope neither of their love languages is Quality Time.

Quality Time also has other dialects, such as doing something together that at least one of you enjoys doing and the other chooses to participate. For the person whose love language is Quality Time, what you are doing is not as important as the fact you are doing it together. It may be planting a garden together. During this season, it may be cleaning out a closet or the garage together. The important thing is that you are choosing to give your full attention to being with your spouse.

Physical Touch—meaningful, affirming touches. In a marriage, this would be such things as holding hands, kissing, embracing, sexual intercourse, placing your hand on their shoulder as you pour their coffee, or putting your hand on their leg as you drive down the road. We have long known the power of physical touch. That is why we cuddle babies in our arms, and long before the baby understands the meaning of love, the baby feels loved by physical touch.

Out of these five love languages, each of us has a primary love language. One of them speaks more deeply to us emotionally than the other four. We can receive love in all five languages, but one is more meaningful. It is very similar to spoken language. Each of us grew up speaking a language with a dialect. That is the one we understand best. We call it our "native tongue." The same is true with love. Some people have said to me, "I think I have two love languages." My response is, "Fine, we will call you bilingual." However, most people have one that is predominant.

Now, don't assume that all men have Physical Touch as their primary love language. I say this because so many men will automatically say, "I know my love language— Physical Touch." They are talking about sexual intercourse. My question to them is, "Do nonsexual touches make you feel loved?" At first, they look at me like a deer in the headlights as if to ask, "Are there nonsexual touches?" Then I ask, "Let's say the two of you are taking a walk, and your wife reaches out and holds your hand. Does that make you feel loved?" If he says, "No, that kind of irritates me when I'm walking." "So," I ask, "Let's say she is pouring you a cup of coffee, and she puts her hand on your shoulder. Does that make you feel loved?" If he says, "Not really." "Well then, Physical Touch is not your love language. You like sex, but touch is not your love language."

The love languages are not gender specific. A man or woman can have any one of the five as their primary love language. The important thing is to discover your spouse's primary love language and choose to speak it on a regular basis. This does not mean that you can ignore the other languages. No, you can sprinkle in the other four for "extra credit." However, if you don't speak your spouse's primary love language, they will not feel loved even though you are speaking some of the other languages. This explains why the wife in the illustration I gave at the beginning of the chapter did not feel loved even though her husband was speaking Acts of Service fluently. Her love language was Quality Time. Remember she said, "We don't ever talk. We haven't talked in twenty years." Her husband was sincere, but sincerity is not enough. We must learn and choose to speak our spouse's primary love language if we want to revitalize our marriage.

So how do you discover your spouse's primary love language? Let me suggest three ways. First, observe their behavior. How do they typically respond to you and other people? If they are always giving gifts to others, that is a clue that their own language is Receiving Gifts. We tend to speak our own love language. If they are often giving others encouraging words, then Words of Affirmation is likely their own love language. Second, observe what they complain about most often. Their complaint reveals their love language. If they say, "I don't think you would ever touch me if I did not initiate it," they are telling you that Physical Touch is their love language. If they say, "I wish I'd at least get some appreciation or thanks every once in a while," they are revealing that Words of Affirmation is their love language. Third, observe what they request most often. Again, the request reveals the love language. If they often say, "Honey, can we take a walk after dinner?" They are asking for Quality Time. If, when you leave the house to go to the grocery store, your spouse says, "Be sure and bring me a surprise," they are telling you that Receiving Gifts is their love language. If you put those three together, you will likely clearly identify the primary love language of your spouse.

Another fun thing you might like to do is take the free online love language quiz at 5lovelanguages.com or the official 5 Love Languages app, Love Nudge, for iOS and Android. You will make thirty choices, and it will show your primary and secondary love languages. You can match the results with what you have discovered in the three observations I have suggested above. There is also a quiz for children and another for teenagers. Imagine what would happen to the family atmosphere if we all discovered each other's love language and began speaking it regularly. This time of confinement may become the best time yet for our marriage and our children.

In this chapter, I have given you information on how

to rekindle love in your marriage. I cannot give you motivation. However, I'm assuming if you have read this far, you are already motivated to revitalize your marriage. Few things are more important than meeting your spouse's emotional need for love. If your spouse has joined you in reading this chapter, you will likely discover each other's love language and begin or continue speaking it daily. If your spouse has not read the chapter and is not interested, don't give up. Remember the power of influence. If you will begin speaking the love language of your spouse and are consistent for the next few months, I predict that you will begin to see a change in the way your spouse relates to you. Love stimulates love. I have seen many marriages revitalized when one spouse was willing to choose to love and express it in the appropriate language. If your emotions push you to think, "I don't have the energy to do this. It probably won't help. They will never change," don't follow your emotions. Choose a positive attitude: "This may help. I don't feel like doing this, but I choose to do it. I am going to do my part in seeking to make my marriage better." I have never known anyone who regretted trying.

MAKING IT PRACTICAL

1. If you already knew your spouse's love language, how faithful have you been in speaking it? Rank yourself on a scale of 0–10. What will you do today to enhance your efforts?

2. If you did not know your spouse's love language, make the three observations suggested in this chapter, and see if it becomes clear. You might also take the free quiz and encourage your spouse to do the same.

3. On a scale of 0–10, how much love do you feel coming from your spouse? Would you be willing to ask your spouse the following questions? On a scale of 0–10, how much love do you feel coming from me? What could I do to raise the score? Their answer will likely tell you their love language, even if they have not read the chapter.

4. If your spouse has read the chapter with you, have a "sit down" talk and listening session to discuss the love languages. Look back over your years together and talk

about why you felt loved or did not feel loved in certain seasons. Can you agree to try to focus on each other's love language during the present crisis?

5. If your spouse has not read the chapter and is not interested, will you make the choice to speak their love language on a regular basis for the next few months and see what happens? Remember the power of influence. Your love may well stimulate their love.

CHAPTER 4

LEARN THE VALUE OF TEAMWORK

Marriage is a team sport. Successful couples learn how to work as a team. Players on an athletic team do not all do the same tasks, but they do have the same objective. Their success is determined largely by how well each person does their part. Marriage is a team of two. We have chosen to process life together. There are hundreds of tasks to be done each week in the normal flow of married life. Most of us remember the early days of marriage when we were deciding who would do what.

Some of our decisions were made based on the model of our parents. If her mother was the primary cook, the wife may have seen that as her role. If the husband's father was the chef, then he may have viewed this as his role. In such cases, we had to negotiate what role each of us would play in food preparation. In my premarital counseling through the years, I have often encouraged couples to make a list of all the things that will need to be done on a regular basis after they get married. If they are diligent, it would be a long list. It would include such things as buying groceries, cooking, washing dishes, vacuuming floors, mopping floors, cleaning toilets, mowing grass, washing cars, keeping gas in the car, paying monthly utility bills, balancing the check book, etc. Then I would encourage each of them to take a copy of the list and privately put their own initials beside the items they thought they would likely do and their fiancé's initials beside those they would expect them to do. If they thought they might do some of the items together, then put both initials, but underline the one who would take the major responsibility.

Once the assignment was completed, we looked at their lists and realized that there were several items where each had put the other's initials. Now it was time for negotiation. I might ask the woman, "Why did you put his initials beside cleaning the toilet?" The most common response was, "Because that is what my dad did." He had envisioned her cleaning the toilets because that is what his mother did. So the obvious question is, "In your marriage, who is going to clean the toilet?" One may quickly volunteer or one may say, "I think we should take turns." Okay, then, "Will you each do it for a month? Or will you do it every other week? And who will take the first week or month?" Obviously, deciding the role each team member will play takes some negotiating. However, the couples that discuss these issues before they get married will have smoother sailing afterwards.

Even when we make these decisions, it does not mean that we will play the same role forever. We may discover after marriage that one team member is more adept at a particular task than another. In my own marriage, we agreed that my wife would pay the monthly utility bills and balance the check book. About four months into marriage, Karolyn asked, "Honey, would you mind taking this responsibility?" I replied, "I could, but why do you ask?" "It hurts my stomach," she said. I was in graduate school, and each of us was working part-time, so it was a rather lean budget. So I understood what she meant. I agreed to take on that task and have been doing it all these years. The ideal is to get each team member in the best place so you can have a winning team.

Now let's get personal. How did the two of you decide the roles you would play on the marriage team? Did you decide before marriage, or did you just work it out as you went along? Many couples look back and admit, "We had some real struggles in this area of our marriage." In fact, some will even admit, "We are still struggling." One may feel that they are carrying a heavier load than their spouse. They see the division of labor as being unfair. Many marital conflicts center on these differing perceptions. (We will talk about a healthy way to resolve conflicts in chapter 5.) But for the moment, let's assume that you have more or less agreed on the role each of you play on the team, and life is going fairly smoothly (or at least, it was!).

Then came COVID-19, and the whole playing field was reconfigured. No longer are you following your morning routine. Neither of you is leaving the house for your job. One of you may be working at home, and the other no longer has a job. Or both of you may be working at home or neither of you has a job. Because one of you is a "night person" and the other a "morning person," one of you may be sleeping later than usual since there is no pressure to get out of bed. You know the feeling—"the world is a different place, and I'm not sure of my role."

If you have children, the playing field is even more confusing. Whoever took the children to school has lost that role. Whoever fixed breakfast for the children may be the one who is now "sleeping in," and the spouse is trying to figure out how to feed hungry children in the morning. If one of you packed a lunch for the children, that job is now gone. Or if they had lunch in the school cafeteria, a new job for parents has just appeared. I could go on, but I don't need to do so. You are living in a new reality, and your role on the team is not nearly as defined as it once was.

This chapter is about going back to the drawing board and rethinking our place on the team. So let me make what I hope are some helpful suggestions. But first, let me suggest that you quiz yourself on how well you are doing with the ideas found in chapters 1–3. So let's review by asking the following questions: Have I called a truce on throwing verbal bombs? Am I focusing on replacing criticism with compliments? If I broke the truce, have I apologized? Am I speaking my spouse's primary love language consistently? Practicing these three skills will create a positive atmosphere in which to discuss your changing roles during this time of adjusting to a new playing field.

Now, as you begin to focus on what roles may need to be adjusted, let me encourage you to begin with questions rather than statements. Note the difference in the two approaches. "Honey, I know that we are both trying to adjust to our new situation. What stresses you the most, and what could I do that might be helpful?" Compare that approach to this: "You have got to take more responsibility with the children. I can't do all of this by myself." The first comes across as loving and the second as demanding. How would you likely respond if your spouse used the loving approach? What might you say if your spouse used the "let me tell you" approach? Questions open the door for your spouse to share their feelings, frustrations, and suggestions of what would be helpful. In statements, you are sharing your own feelings and frustrations, but they likely hit your spouse broadside and stimulate defensiveness. Don't get me wrong, your spouse needs to know how you feel, but first you need to make sure their door is open to hearing. Your model of asking questions and extending the desire to help your spouse will create an atmosphere in which they are more likely to ask you the same question.

Before the "shelter-in-place" order was given, Dot's accepted role was to prepare breakfast for the family. Then she would leave for work. Her husband, Rob, would help the children get dressed and drive them to school on his way to work. Everything worked smoothly. Dot was not a "morning person," but she accepted her role without complaining. However, now that no one was leaving the house in the mornings, she preferred to sleep in a little later. Yet the children were up and ready for breakfast on their normal schedule. She was feeling a little frustrated at not being able to enjoy one of the benefits of home confinement. When Rob asked her, "Where are you feeling most stressed, and what could I do to help you?" She immediately told him what she was feeling and wondered if he could fix breakfast for the children during this time. Rob is a "morning person," so he readily agreed. Dot said to him, "You have got to be the greatest husband in the world." Rob's love language is Words of Affirmation, so his love tank shot from a seven to a ten. If Rob had not asked the question, Dot may have held her frustration inside for another week or so and then exploded with such words as, "I don't know why you couldn't fix breakfast for the children and let me sleep a little later. I am really frustrated." The story may not have had a happy ending.

My second suggestion is: take time to evaluate your personality differences. We all know that we have different patterned ways of responding to life. We have just discussed "morning people" and "night people." I have sometimes called this the "Robin" and the "Owl." The Robin rises early and alert ("The early bird gets the worm"), while the Owl is awake and active at night, but come morning, the "do not disturb" sign is on the door. Respecting these differences, and not trying to change the other person, makes for a positive atmosphere. The goal is to look for ways in which your differences can work for your marriage, not against it. That is exactly what Dot and Rob did in the illustration above.

Another personality difference is the "Neatnik" and the "Slob." "A place for everything and everything in its place" is the theme of the Neatnik, while the Slob's most asked question is: "Where is it?" The sooner we learn that some people are not wired to keep up with their car keys, the sooner we will have a winning team. Don't try to force them into being a Neatnik by putting a hook in the garage and expecting them to hang their keys on it. It will not happen. One husband said, "I attached her keys to a tennis ball. I knew she could not misplace the tennis ball. I was wrong." Far better to get three sets of keys and say, "Use these, Honey, I'll find the others later." And you will (perhaps in the refrigerator). Be there for each other. Play to each other's strengths. Consider personality differences while you try to find the right place for each team member on this new playing field.

My third suggestion is to discover your spouse's passion and help them attain it. Maggie had majored in English in college, and in her earlier years, she aspired to be an author. However, after marriage, her day job took most of her energy, and the idea of writing was put on the back burner. Then came the baby, and then another. When COVID-19 struck, the children were in first and third grades. Maggie had a steady rhythm in her life, and she and Kevin had a good relationship. However, there still was little time for writing. One afternoon when Kevin was playing in the yard with the children, she sat down at the computer and started writing. She wrote an article on the joys of being a mother when Mom and Dad are on the same team. She printed it and laid it on the desk intending to proofread it later. That night after Kevin put the children to bed, he picked it up and read it. "This is a great article, Maggie," he said. "Oh, you read it? Did you really like it?" "I loved it," he said. "You need to submit this to the local newspaper." That was the encouragement she needed. She did submit it, and the next week it was published. Who knows what she will write next, but it all started in the midst of a pandemic because Kevin encouraged her.

Most of us have ideas of things we would like to do or accomplish in life. You probably know what is in your own mind, but do you know what is in the mind of your spouse? If you don't already know, this would be a good time to ask, "If you could do anything in the world, what would you like to do?" They may have more than one idea. Helping your spouse succeed in reaching their goals brings one of life's deepest satisfactions. Remember, you are a team; when one of you succeeds, you both succeed. You could take the first step, even in the midst of the present situation.

MAKING IT PRACTICAL

1. Before COVID-19, were you satisfied with the role each of you was playing on the team? If not, what would you have liked to change?

2. Since the pandemic, what changes have you made in your roles? What changes would you like to discuss with your spouse?

3. Ask your spouse: "In the midst of all the changes that are taking place, what do you find most stressful, and what could I do to be helpful?"

4. What personality differences do you find most annoying? How could you make those differences work for you rather than divide you?

5. Ask your spouse: "When you think of life, what would you really like to do or accomplish?" Then ask: "What could I do to help you accomplish that goal?"

CHAPTER 5

HAVE A DAILY "SIT DOWN AND LISTEN" TIME

We often say, "Let's sit down and talk," but most of us need to learn to listen. Now obviously, if listening is going to take place, someone needs to be talking. However, many of us have never learned how to listen empathetically. Empathy focuses on trying to understand the thoughts and feelings of the one who is talking. It is mentally trying to put yourself in their shoes and see the world through their eyes. By nature, we are not listening to understand, but to respond. While they are talking, we are thinking about what we are going to say, rather than trying to understand what they are saying.

For many years, I have encouraged couples to have a "daily sharing time" in which each of them shares "three things that happened in my life today and how I feel about them." It is a way of staying in touch with each other in the business of life. Many couples have found this to be an extremely helpful way of staying connected.

Now that you are confined to close quarters, you may wonder why this would be necessary. The reality is, you cannot read each other's minds. You may observe your spouse sorting the laundry, but you do not know what they are thinking or feeling. We can be in the same house and still feel miles apart. When you make time to listen to your spouse, you are communicating that you value your relationship. If you do not presently have a "daily sharing time," let me encourage you to start one. If you have children, this will be more difficult, but in many ways even more important for your marriage. It can be when the baby is napping or after the children have gone to bed, but make time for what you believe to be important.

The "daily sharing time" is for the purpose of staying mentally and emotionally connected. However, in this chapter, I want to focus on how to stay connected when we have conflicts. In my forty plus years of counseling couples, most of their unresolved conflicts are the result of a failure to genuinely understand each other. Understanding only comes with empathetic listening. Conflicts are inevitable. There are no couples that do not have conflicts. Why is that true? Because we are humans, and humans do not have the same thoughts and feelings. We are uniquely made. We see the world and our situation through different eyes. We have emotions that our spouse does not have, even when we are facing the same circumstances.

During the present "social distancing" environment, you and your spouse may well be responding very differently. One of you may feel anxious, fearful, or even depressed, while the other is upbeat, hopeful, and even peaceful. We are influenced by our personalities and our history. Trudy grew up in a home that was very unstable. Her parents often argued, and when she was thirteen, her father left and never returned. Her mother struggled even to keep food on the table and was often depressed. It is easy to understand why Trudy might feel extremely anxious in the present environment. Her husband, John, grew up in a stable home where his mom and dad had a loving, supportive relationship. In times of difficulty, they worked together as a team, and John always felt secure. Again, our present state of mind is influenced by our history. We cannot expect our spouse to respond to the present situation in the same manner as we do.

In the present environment, you may be discovering new areas of conflict that you had not encountered when things were more stable. Ted and Rachel found themselves in a heated argument about letting the children spend the weekend with Rachel's parents, who lived across town. Rachel was feeling the need for some emotional reprieve from her 24/7 duty as a mom. Ted, on the other hand, was resistant because her mother already had some physical challenges, and he knew that she had been sneaking out and going to the home of her hairdresser while the shop was closed. He argued that she may well have been exposed to the virus because other people were also going to the home of the hairdresser. Perhaps you have discovered your own "new" conflict areas.

A conflict is not simply a difference of opinion. He prefers salmon and she prefers chicken. That is not a conflict but merely a preference. A conflict is when the two of you disagree about something, and you both feel strongly that the other person is wrong. Conflicts typically lead to arguments, and arguments usually make things worse. He says that she is selfish, and she says that he is irresponsible. The argument gets hot as they lash out at each other. Eventually, one of them walks out and slams the door. The conflict is now swept under the rug and remains unresolved. When a couple sweeps conflicts under the rug, eventually they begin to say to themselves, "We are not compatible. We don't agree on anything. This is never going to work. I've got to get out of this marriage." The reality is, they are two humans who never learned to resolve conflicts. I want to share some basic ideas on how to solve conflicts and thus build a healthy marriage.

At the heart of solving conflicts is developing the practice of empathetic listening, which we discussed above. However, most couples will not learn this skill without a plan. So let's first agree with each other that we would prefer to solve our conflicts rather than argue. That should not be a hard decision to make. Then let's establish a weekly "sit down and listen" time to process one conflict (only one per week). That's fifty-two a year. That should be adequate. The first guideline is to take turns talking.

One of you will take five minutes and share "your side," your perspective. At the end of five minutes, the listener may ask questions to clarify what they heard you saying, such as, "What I understood you to say is. . . . Is that correct?" Ask as many clarifying questions as you like, but don't respond with your opinion. Remember, you are now the "listener." When the "talker" says, "Yes, that is what I am saying, and that is how I feel," your response is extremely important. You affirm their thoughts and feelings. (This does not mean that you necessarily agree with their perspective.) You might say, "I think I understand what you are saying, and I can see how that makes sense. And I can see why you would feel disappointed (or whatever emotion they have expressed)." With this statement, you are no longer an enemy; you are their friend.

Now it is time for you to have your five minutes as the "talker." You might begin by saying, "So let me share my perspective. Hopefully you can understand where I'm coming from." Your spouse now becomes the "listener" who does not interrupt you but listens with a desire to truly understand your thoughts and feelings. At the end of your turn, they may ask clarifying questions to make sure they understand what you are thinking and feeling.

Then they verbally affirm you. "I understand what you are saying, and I can see how it makes sense. I think I can also see why you would feel hurt." We have not yet solved the conflict, but we have created an emotional climate in which we can focus on finding a solution rather than trying to win an argument.

Remember Ted and Rachel, who were conflicted about allowing the children to spend the weekend with her parents? When they genuinely listened to each other's perspective, Ted was able to say, "I can see that it would be really good for you to have a break. I understand how you could feel exhausted." She was able to say, "I understand what you are saying, and I can see how you would be fearful." The next question was, "So what are we going to do?" They began discussing possibilities. They ended by agreeing that on Saturday, Ted would spend the day with the children. He would fix breakfast and then pack a picnic lunch. He would take the children on a ride in the countryside and see how many cows they could see. Then they would take a hike in the woods behind their house. Rachel could spend the day resting or doing whatever she chooses to do without being concerned about the children. The solution was not what either of them originally had in mind, but it worked for both of them, and the children loved the idea.

Often the resolution of conflicts requires compromise. We find a meeting place, somewhere between our two original ideas, on which we both agree. In other conflicts, one of us may agree to go with the other spouse's original idea. For example, Susan and George, with reduced income, were trying to decide what could be eliminated from their budget. Susan thought that George should cancel his membership at the local fitness center. Her reasoning was that he was not able to use the membership presently because of the threat of infection, and the monthly fee was significant. George was reluctant to do so because he was hoping he would be able to utilize the facility soon. After their "sit down and listen" session, George agreed to go with Susan's suggestion, and he did so without resentment.

Some conflicts are more difficult to resolve. We can hear, understand, and affirm each other and still not be able to come to an agreement. On those occasions, we agree to disagree for the moment, while we each give thought to possible solutions. We may discuss it again next week or next month, depending on how time sensitive the issue is. In the meantime, our relationship is not fractured by the conflict, because we both love and affirm each other. In the midst of the present situation, Bill had shared with Rebecca that he was thinking this might be a good time for him to consider retirement. After all, he was retirement age, and he was not sure when he would be able to go back to work, or even if he would have a job after the crises is over. The thought of retirement put Rebecca into a state of panic. After the present confinement to home, she was not sure she was ready for Bill to be home all the time. They had not learned how to listen empathetically, so they had a rather heated argument, after which they did not talk to each other much for the next few days. Had they followed the suggestions in this book, they may well have been able to understand each other's thoughts and feelings and affirmed each other. Their conclusion may well have been "let's agree to disagree" at the moment and discuss it again in a month. Having reached this agreement, they could continue to be kind and supportive of each other.

Conflicts can be resolved. We may not agree with each other, but we can find a workable solution with which we can live in harmony. I hope the ideas we have discussed will help you as you perhaps face some conflicts you had not faced before the crisis. Remember, the key is to listen to each other empathically with a view to understanding and affirming their thoughts and feelings. A "daily sharing time" and a "weekly conflict-resolution time" both require a "sit down and listen" mentality.

MAKING IT PRACTICAL

1. If you already have a "daily sharing time," focus on learning to listen empathetically.

   When your spouse is talking, try to see things through their eyes. Don't focus on what you are thinking but on trying to understand their thoughts and feelings.

2. If you do not have a daily "sit down and listen" time, ask your spouse if they would be willing to try it. You might start with a time limit of ten or fifteen minutes. Each of you will share two or three things that happened today and how you felt. Remember, the purpose is to understand what the other person is thinking and feeling, and thus stay connected. Do not use this time to condemn your spouse for something they said or did.

3. Consider trying a "weekly conflict-resolution time" that will focus on one conflict you have encountered recently. Focus on learning how to listen empathetically and verbally affirming the perspective and feelings of your spouse. Try taking turns as "the talker" and "the listener."

4. If you are experiencing a number of conflict areas, make a list and rank them in order of importance. Let your spouse do the same. Then every other week, each of you can choose the topic for the week. Explore the three ways to resolve a conflict: finding a compromise that works for both of you, one spouse agreeing to go with the other's desire, or simply agreeing to disagree at the moment.

5. In the past, how successful have you been in resolving conflicts? What steps could you take to make conflict resolution a more positive experience?

EPILOGUE

Whatever your situation looks like, I hope you will utilize the five suggestions we have discussed to revitalize your marriage. Don't submit to the thoughts and feelings that things are hopeless. This is the time to push into your marriage, not a time to become passive. Even if your spouse is not willing to read the book or discuss these ideas, there is still hope. It is true that one person cannot create a healthy marriage, but one person can take the first step. If you seek to implement these ideas, you can create a more positive emotional climate. What you say and do will always influence your spouse, either in a positive or negative manner. I want to encourage you to seek to make it a positive influence. Even if your spouse does not have a positive response, you will feel better about yourself. You will know that you did the right thing in the midst of the storm.

There is significance to the order of the above chapters. If we don't begin with a truce on throwing verbal bombs, the marriage is not likely to get better. As long as we are in warfare, we will not have peace. When the bombs stop dropping, we can then apologize for our failures, past and present. Hopefully our spouse will forgive us, but at least we have torn the wall down on our side. Then, when we discover and speak our spouse's love language, we are addressing their deepest emotional need—the need to feel loved. When we get love flowing in both directions, we are much more likely to learn the value of teamwork. We definitely need to be a team when the strong waves of uncertainty are pushing against our ship. A daily "sit down and listen" time will help us maintain a loving, supportive relationship. A weekly (or whenever needed) "sit down and listen" time that focuses on resolving our conflicts will help us continue to face the storms of life in a healthy manner.

If you have found these ideas helpful, I hope you will

share them with your friends. Together we can help create an environment for healthy marriages and a safe haven for children. The storms of life are inevitable, but shipwreck is avoidable.

Note
1. Proverbs 18:21a.

STAY CONNECTED
and take the next step . . .

BOOK

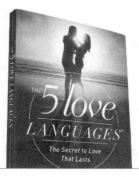

ONLINE

5lovelanguages.com

APP